From
SEGREGATION
to INTEGRATION

Growing Up and Living Black in the South

Mary Cuthbertson Blakeney

FROM SEGREGATION TO INTEGRATION
GROWING UP AND LIVING BLACK IN THE SOUTH

iUniverse books may be ordered through booksellers or by contacting:

iUniverse
1663 Liberty Drive
Bloomington, IN 47403
www.iuniverse.com
1-800-Authors (1-800-288-4677)

ISBN: 978-1-5320-6194-3 (sc)
ISBN: 978-1-5320-6193-6 (e)

Library of Congress Control Number: 2018913285

Print information available on the last page.

iUniverse rev. date: 11/09/2018

To the memory of my mother, Sallie Cuthbertson, who loved me unconditionally. She worked two jobs to provide for the two of us and to pay for my college education. I know she was proud of my success and has smiled many times as she has viewed after death my participation in the community after I retired.

To my son, Daman, who is a very loving, caring, and intelligent person. He has made his father and me very proud.

To my husband, Benjamin, my loving, thoughtful, and helpful partner in a very happy marriage. To God be the glory!

CONTENTS

INTRODUCTION

I want people to know that though there are differences between black and white people, they are far outweighed by the likenesses they share. Africans and their African American descendants are the only people who were originally brought to this country against their will. Consequently, they have been—and, to a certain extent, are still—denied complete civil rights. All other people who make up the melting pot of America migrated here for the freedom they did not have as they desired in Europe and elsewhere. Africans were forced to leave their countries and the freedom they enjoyed for imprisonment in a country that valued only their labor.

Black Americans bleed the same blood types as do whites; cry the same kind of tears when sad or hurt; and have the same needs for food, shelter, currency, and education. Most important, they have the same capacity to think, learn, love, and pray as do their white counterparts. The color of their skin sets them apart from other races and nationalities of people, and for that they do not apologize.

PREFACE

As I sat relaxing and watching television news and reading newspaper accounts about the removal of the Confederate flag (January to May 2000) from the South Carolina capitol dome, I thought real progress was being made toward integration.

Fast-forward to July 10, 2015, when Dylann Roof shot and killed nine African Americans in Emanuel AME Church in Charleston, South Carolina. The Confederate flag was removed from the capitol grounds of South Carolina. This was another giant step in removing a symbol of segregation.

That said, in 1993, I was walking one morning in the historic district of Concord, North Carolina, which was predominately white. I observed a white female gathering cleaning supplies from her car; she was about to clean someone's house. I thought perhaps she owned a cleaning business or worked for one. I thought about the years during segregation when black women were the cleaning ladies and they had to enter the homes of the white people they worked for through the back doors.

Until I was about twenty-eight, I lived and worked in a segregated society along with millions of fellow Americans of African descent. We were always separated from whites because of laws implemented by the lawmakers who were white.

═══ CHAPTER 1 ═══

Segregation as I Lived It

I lived in the small city of Concord in Cabarrus County in North Carolina. It has grown tremendously over the years, but before the mid-1960s, it was just another segregated part of the South. Today, people who have not had to endure the restraints of segregation have a hard time understanding what it was like.

There were two theaters downtown for whites, the Paramount and Cabarrus. The Cabarrus allowed blacks to sit in the balcony, but the refreshments were limited because the closet-like booth where the tickets were sold had only a small space. Black moviegoers were not subjected to a white person selling tickets; usually, a black person handled that. My aunt Fredonia Murphy Russell worked there for a time. The only time a white person was in the booth was when the regular person was not able to make it.

The balcony was always clean, and the seats were nicely upholstered, the duplicate of the first floor. Of course, we did not learn that until after integration. There were times when a movie was very popular and more black people wanted to see it than could be accommodated in the balcony, so they would have to wait for the second showing or go back the next night.

Eventually, some white person realized money could be made in the African American community. Two new structures on the same street were built to house the Roxy and Lincoln Theaters, and movies were shown on the weekends. The theaters were across from each other on Lincoln Street, with a distance of approximately five hundred feet in between. They were so close that if you were walking up to one theater, you could see who was approaching the other.

As a people who did not knowing anything other than segregation, we thought that was the greatest thing since sweet potato pie. Of course, all the actors in the movies were white, and for the most part, these two theaters usually showed westerns and none of the cowboys were black. However, history tells us there were African American cowboys. The classic drama movies were shown downtown at the Cabarrus or the Paramount. There was never a time I can remember that either of the theaters in the neighborhood was filled to capacity as was the Cabarrus.

The few African Americans who were actors got roles in classics such as *Gone with the Wind* and *Song of the South*. Hattie McDaniel said, "I'd rather be paid to play a maid than paid to be a maid. The pay is better." She was the first African American to win an Oscar (1940) from the Academy of Motion Pictures, Arts, and Sciences. She was voted Best Supporting Actress for her performance in *Gone with the Wind*.

A soda shop adjacent to the Roxy was owned and operated by Andrew Handy Sr. and his family. Mr. Handy had worked at one of the drugstores delivering prescriptions on the store's motorcycle before that. Drugstores sold Cokes, milkshakes, sandwiches, candy, cigarettes, and the like primarily to white people. We could only stand at the counter and wait endlessly depending on the temperament of the white person to buy anything. If we were able to make a purchase, we had to take it with us. Many times, we would tire of waiting and being ignored and just leave. So to have a soda shop owned by an African American in our community made our lives more enjoyable. There were stools at the counter, booths along one wall, and room to dance to the jukebox's music. Handy's was frequented mostly by teenagers, but adults would go in to get a sandwich and a soda or just spend time talking to Mr. Handy before the teens arrived.

We attended Logan High School, a union school (grades one through twelve) just as all others were then. It was in a segregated community, and we walked to school. Schoolmates who passed Handy's on the way home stopped to listen to records on the jukebox and buy sodas. It was the gathering place after school. I, however, lived in the opposite direction from Handy's and wasn't allowed to go there after school. I had chores to do, but like teens do, I broke the rules a few times, but I would stay only a few minutes and then rush home to play catch-up. I finally realized that little bit of fun wasn't worth the risk—my mother passed there on her way home from work, and I knew I could be caught.

I could, however, go there after athletic events and on the weekends. I told my mother about breaking her rule only after I was in college. She smiled and shook her head. Years later, I told my teenage son about that. I wanted him to know that some teens were defiant at times but that others were smarter about shaping up and obeying their parents' rules.

Handy's was always overflowing on the weekends and during holidays with teens from Concord, Kannapolis, and Charlotte. Even some who had graduated from high school would come around because it was a place to find familiar people.

CHAPTER 2

Growing Up

To give you a better understanding of how I grew up, I will start with my childhood. My mother, Sallie Cuthbertson, was a solo parent; we lived with my grandparents Callie and James Cuthbertson, who had adopted her. Her birth mother, Estelle Bost, remained in her life until her death in 1972.

I was about eight or nine before I really knew who Estelle was because she was not living in Concord. Mama Estelle, as my mother and I called her, lived in Wilmington, Delaware. She moved there because she was able to earn more money working there than she would have in Concord.

I was close to Mama Callie and loved her dearly; she spoiled me but also disciplined me. For Christmas one year, I got a blackboard and chalk as most children did then. She taught me the alphabet and numbers. I had a red rocking chair (which I still have) I would sit in beside the blackboard while Mama Callie would point to the letters and numbers, telling me what they were. As time passed and she felt I knew the letters and numbers, she'd go over them with me. If I missed one, she would pop me lightly with a little hickory switch. She didn't work, so we were together all day while my grandfather and mother worked.

Mama Callie spoiled me just enough so that I would whine when my mother did things like wash my hair; I wanted my grandmother to do that. I wasn't allowed to become a spoiled brat by any stretch of the imagination, however.

Unfortunately, Mama Callie died when I was five, but I remember some of the things she did, such as making delicious cakes, pies, and bread. I didn't like green beans and green peas, but she made me eat them anyway; I couldn't leave the table until I did. There were days, however, that my aunt Jessie Reid Bost would stop at our house on her way home to see Mama Callie, her sister. When Aunt Jessie would see I was still at the table with those green beans or peas on the plate, she would help me get rid of them by eating them herself or telling me to go out on the back porch and throw them away while she made noises so no one would know what was going on. When I was older, we laughed about the tricks we played on Mama Callie. Aunt Jessie was the adult the children in the family could talk to and have the most fun with.

After Mama Callie died, my mother and I lived alone because Grandpa Jim had moved to Washington, DC. We never received public assistance or handouts of any kind. Public assistance then wasn't available as it is today. Other children and I learned about the Great Depression and how black folks had to find ways to survive as best they could from our families and neighbors; we were too young to know what was happening.

My mother said that Grandpa Jim and other men would go over to the train tracks to pick up coal that had fallen off the trains as they passed through when they didn't have money to buy it. African American men didn't earn a lot of money, so we had not much to live on. Anyone with any savings had spent it during the Depression because people were out of work, and black men made up the largest number of the unemployed.

Grandpa Jim, who moved to Washington, DC, worked at the Navy Yard in Maryland until his health failed. He died in 1962. He helped produce equipment for the space capsule that took Scott Carpenter into space. That was the capsule that landed in the ocean on its return to earth. Scott Carpenter was rescued before it sank, and later, the capsule was retrieved from the ocean.

Mama Estelle was the mother of three daughters—Ether, Sallie, and Fredonia. She decided to allow Ether and Sallie to be adopted, and she reared Fredonia herself. Ether grew up in Virginia and didn't get to know Sallie or Fredonia very well. I remember seeing her only once when she came to Concord. She married and had two girls whom I have never seen.

Our blood relatives—the Loves, Bosts, and some Asburys—seemed more like friends because my mother and I didn't get to know them very well while I was growing up. We became more familiar with them as we attended gatherings such as camp meetings at Ebenezer AME Zion Church in Midland, North Carolina, or seeing them at other public gatherings.

During the late 1970s and 1980s, family reunions were held, and we got to know other relatives better. Since students were bused to Logan High School from Cabarrus County, this was another way we got acquainted with our relatives.

As far back as I can remember, we always had plenty of food, and other families did as well. When neighbors, friends, or family stopped by to visit during the holidays or on Sundays at dinner, we always had more than enough food to share.

Sharing seemed to be the common thread during segregation; it helped black people survive.

On Easter, Thanksgiving, and Christmas, there were extra desserts prepared for our indulgence. At Christmas, the traditional coconut cake was made with fresh coconut. Getting to the white flesh of the coconut was not easy. First, holes were made in what looked like eyes to allow the milk to drain from the coconut. Then the shell was cracked with a hammer. A knife was then used to pry the flesh out of the hard shell. The flesh had a brown covering on it that we peeled off with a knife; we then grated the flesh. When I was old enough, it was my task to get the coconut ready and grate it for the cake. I never liked the taste of coconut, so after doing all the work, I never ate any. Another cake was baked for me such as a pound cake or a pineapple cake.

For Easter and Thanksgiving, there might be sweet potato or peach pies in addition to a cake of some kind. Because mothers in black families gathered fruits and vegetables and canned them during the summer, there was always something to use for dinners during the fall, winter, and early spring. However, Sunday meals were the largest of the week.

Because there were no regulations forbidding cows, pigs, chickens and other fowl, or horses, many of these animals were found throughout the communities both black and white. The land behind our houses extended beyond the property lines and was vacant. The hog pens and barns were far enough away from the houses so their odors didn't cause a problem as they would today. Neighbors who had cows would sell milk and butter to those who wanted it. The horses and mules were used to plow gardens for neighbors and white folks. Those were ways that families could earn money.

When one family killed hogs, the men in the neighborhood would help because they knew they would need the same favor. There was plenty of work to do not only on the day of the killing but also for the next two or three days to preserve the meat. They ground meat for sausage and liver mush, salted the fatback, and salted and peppered the hams for curing. The chitterlings of course had to be cleaned and cooked. All the hard work paid off when the meats were eaten throughout the winter. The excess fat was used to make lye soap. My family didn't have hogs, but we would help relatives who lived on the same street.

There was a pantry or a designated place in our homes where all the jars of canned fruits and vegetables were stored. During the summer when crops were plentiful, the women busied themselves canning corn, tomatoes, peaches, apples, okra, green beans, and pickled cucumbers. Most anything that could be put in a jar was; that ensured us that we would have food for the winter and early spring that we did not have to buy at a grocery store. Frankly, there wouldn't have been enough money to do so.

Nearly all families had gardens in their backyards; some were larger than others and had a greater variety of vegetables. Produce from the gardens was eaten, shared with neighbors, or canned. Vendors both white and black would come through the community selling truckloads of fruits and vegetables every week.

I remember Mr. Miles (I refer to him as "Mister" because I never knew his first name), a black man who came from South Carolina about twice a month with a truckload of watermelons, cantaloupes, and peaches. He would sell everything he had because his fruit was so good. Vendors like him provided a way for people who didn't have gardens to grow fruits and vegetables. Some neighbors had peach and pear trees in their yards, but there were times when they didn't bear enough fruit for canning. We had a peach tree for many years that produced only enough peaches for a few pies during the summer.

During the canning process, everyone in the household who was old enough to do something had a job. Older children helped their mothers wash, peel, and cut fruits and vegetables, while the younger ones shucked corn and washed jars and lids in boiling water to sterilize them. Peeling fruits, shucking corn, and snapping green beans happened on porches because there was no air conditioning back then; the coolest place to work was outside. We took advantage of the cool air before going into the kitchen to build a fire that started the canning process. We parboiled the vegetables and fruits before putting them in the sterilized jars with lids that would seal tightly to prevent spoilage. We could tell if the lids were sealed because there would be a popping sound as the jars cooled.

Most African Americans who grew up during segregation are quick to say that they were poor but didn't know it. A few families were better off than others; they were able to buy homes rather than rent because their fathers most likely worked two jobs. My family rented until I graduated from college.

Our home was heated with coal- and wood-burning stoves and kerosene heaters. Using wood and coal helped reduce the cost. Coal cost more than wood, so once the fire was burning and the house was warm, we put in wood to keep the fire burning, so we saved on coal. These were Warm Morning heaters because coal was added before bedtime with the damper closed to allow for slower burning. This was called banking the fire so it did not go out during the night.

During the night, we slept under quilts and blankets on our beds. In the morning, we stoked the red embers, added more coal and a piece of wood, and opened the damper to build a roaring fire that would in a short time warm the room.

To cook, we had our choice of a wood or a kerosene stove. For breakfast, we lit the kerosene stove with a match, and it produced heat quicker, and small kerosene heaters were used in the bedrooms to provide heat while we dressed. These heaters were like the Kerosuns we have today. We used the wood-burning stove to cook large meals when there was plenty of time to make the fire. That stove had a tank on the side that held water, which was heated as the fire burned. We used that to clean the dishes.

We children had the chore of bringing in coal, wood, and kindling from a place under our home or a shed we stored those items in to keep them dry. There was no fire in the house during the day when no one was there. Entering a cold house and having to start a fire wearing your coat until the place got warm was not pleasant, but back then, we didn't have any other way to heat our homes. The portable kerosene heaters were lit first to provide heat as the coal-burning heater got hot. After we got home from watching the Christmas parade downtown, we would be nearly frozen, but the kerosene heater provided much-needed warmth until the Warm Morning heater began to heat up. Some homes in the community had fireplaces, but they were not used because the heat did not flow out into the room.

We had to use tin washtubs and a washboard to do laundry. During winter, it was hard to wash all the clothes at one time because they would freeze if hung outside on the clothesline. In households where the mothers worked all day, washing took place at night and the clothes would be hung on the back porches weather permitting. My mother would send the sheets, towels, and heavy clothing to the laundry to be wet washed or dry washed. We would put those items in a drawstring laundry bag that had our name and address on it. Our request was for a dry wash, and it was usually returned in two to three days.

There was one drawback to the process; the items were terribly wrinkled from being stuffed into the laundry bag right out of the hot dryer because there was no folding, but it was an affordable way of getting our towels and bedding washed during the winter. If we experienced warm winter days, we could wash on Saturdays and hang the laundry on the clotheslines in the backyard. Saturdays were very busy with housecleaning and grocery shopping that had to be done as well.

═══ CHAPTER 3 ═══

The Role of the Church in the African American Community

The churches in the African American community provided more than spirituality; they were information and socialization centers as well. It didn't matter what the denomination was—children were taken to church by their parents until they were old enough to go alone for youth activities. Youth choirs sang on designated Sundays, and junior ushers carried out their duties on the same day.

As children, we looked forward to the Christmas and Easter programs directed by the Christian education director. The director would bring us together nearly a month before the holiday and distribute the parts we were to memorize. We rehearsed on Saturdays so that it did not interfere with school.

After the Christmas program, everyone in attendance received a bag of apples, oranges, tangerines, nuts, and candy prepared by the Sunday school teachers in the Christian education department. We children looked forward to that because we would add those goodies to those we got at home, and they lasted until school started after the holidays.

The annual Easter egg hunt was held on Easter Monday at the church. We looked forward to that; it became a contest to see who could find the most eggs. Our teachers would not let any child go home without eggs, so those who found the most were asked to share, and they were always eager to do so.

In the summer, we would go on what was called a Sunday school picnic. Our transportation was a truck with a wooden flatbed with slats on three sides and a slatted closure on the back like a gate, just like the type that hauls boxes and trash we sometimes see today. Everyone would climb on the truck carrying picnic lunches in baskets and bags, and the back was closed and locked so no one would fall out. The church provided a few stools or chairs for older people, but other than that, there was nothing to sit on, so we stood in one spot until we arrived at the site. It was a balancing act as the truck made turns or went around curves; we would lean against other people. We worked together so that no one fell.

In the South back then, there were very few parks for black people, so we usually went to an area where there was a pond or lake that someone in our community knew about; the owner allowed us to use the pond or lake for our picnics. Of course, we took a softball and a bat. Other activities included singing and playing games that didn't require any equipment. Our parents, Sunday school teachers, church members, and those who were not members from the community looked forward to the yearly trip.

═══ CHAPTER 4 ═══

Life in the Community

Getting an education during segregation was a major priority for African Americans. Though many parents may not have graduated from high school or may not have learned to read and write, they encouraged their children not to make the same mistake. All children were expected to attend school, do their best, and respect their teachers. If we misbehaved in school, our parents would discipline us when they learned about it.

Our parents taught us to respect all adults in the community as well. If we were misbehaving away from home, other adults would correct us, and we knew not to disrespect them. The entire village helped raise the children. This reference wasn't known until black people began the intense study of their roots beginning in the late 1960s.

There was no organized recreation for us back then, so we came up with our own. In the spring, parents and their children played softball together. We would go to a vacant lot near Buffalo Creek, which had a wire bridge suspended from poles, one wire on top and the other on the bottom parallel to each other. To cross the creek, we would have to be tall enough to reach the top wire while standing on the bottom wire and slide our hands and feet across the wires. We kids were not allowed to go to that area to play without adult supervision.

The men used grass slings and scythes for cutting the grass because the push mowers couldn't cut the tall grass and brush in that area. The older children played with the parents, and the younger ones watched, cheered, and kept score. The games were similar to pickup basketball games.

There were few telephones in the neighborhood, so messages about the games were passed orally as the grown-ups were on their way home from work. Whoever had the ball and bat brought them, rocks were used for bases, and scores were written in the dirt or on a paper bag. We would play until nearly dark once or twice a week with our parents.

We children would play together when our parents were too tired or decided they had had enough. When we played in the street, we used rubber balls so we would not break windows. At times, the balls would go into the yards of some neighbors who were not eager to let us get them back, and so we have to find another ball before we could play again.

When the city of Concord began recreation programs, we played at Logan High School's gymnasium and playground. Mr. Jessie C. Banner Sr. was employed to supervise there during the summer. Gradually, a few organized activities such as softball and baseball started up. The gym was open for pickup basketball games as well. The city had already built a swimming pool on Lincoln Street for us also. After many years, it fell into disrepair and was finally removed. There was also a swimming pool downtown behind the original public library. It was integrated in the late 1960s, so we were able to use it until both structures were torn down and replaced with a parking lot.

Many years later, the city of Concord built the McGinnis Aquatic Center near the Academy Recreation Center on Academy Street. However, it was not a regulation swimming pool—it was more or less a wading pool.

The new Cabarrus County Library was built on North Union Street across from where the old swimming pool had been. The new library provided the Bookmobile that traveled throughout the county so residents could have access to books.

CHAPTER 5

Segregated Schools

The only public school in Concord for African Americans was Logan, named for Reverend Frank Thomas Logan. He was a college chaplain, church minister, school principal, and father of five. For forty-nine years, he ran Logan School, which later became Logan High School, a longtime fixture in the southwest part of Concord. That area was known as Coleburg in the 1800s, and it later became known as Logan in honor of the man who had worked so hard for himself and his family and for the intellectual and spiritual growth of the community.

Mr. Logan was born into slavery in Guilford County just before the Civil War, and he came to Concord in 1889 to become chaplain at Scotia Seminary for Colored Women (later the Barber-Scotia College, a four-year, coed liberal arts college). Mr. Logan was educated at Lincoln University in Pennsylvania and graduated from there in 1881. He obtained a theological degree at Lincoln University in 1884. His hometown was Greensboro, North Carolina. He died on August 19, 1945. According to his descendants, he was a man driven to learn and teach, and he pushed his children to do the same.

For many years, Logan had grades one through eleven. Once the twelfth grade was added, I was told many people went back and completed the twelfth year. I also learned that there were several one-room elementary schools in Cabarrus County before Shankletown Elementary was built. When that school opened, the one-room schools were closed and their students were bused to the new elementary school until they completed eighth grade.

Grace Lutheran Church had a school on Chestnut Avenue that consisted of grades one through six. Prior to that, Emanuel Lutheran College and Grace Lutheran School were on Corban Avenue. Eventually the college moved to another city and the elementary school was moved to a building on Chestnut Avenue. Once the children completed sixth grade, they enrolled in Logan to complete their education.

There were two school systems—Concord City and Cabarrus County. Because of segregation, no black children could attend any of the county schools. Once black students completed eighth grade at Shankletown School, they were bused to Logan High to complete grades nine through twelve. They rode past all the white elementary and high schools to get to Shankletown Elementary and Logan High every day; they would leave home early in the dark mornings during the winter and return late in the afternoon. We were the first victims of busing.

I was a student at Logan from grades one through twelve. Students who lived in the county could not participate in sports because they lacked transportation home after practice and games. However, that didn't limit Logan High's participation in football and basketball. If some of the students from the county wanted to participate badly enough, they would move in with relatives who lived in the city.

The teams were the Tigers and Tigerettes. Mr. Jessie C. Banner Sr. served as the head football and basketball coach and athletic director. Mr. Thomas E. Galloway and Miss Vivian Freeman coached girls' basketball. However, when I was a freshman on the team, the coach was Miss Edwards. She left to take a job at another school. During my senior year on the basketball team, we won the Consolation and Sportsmanship Awards and I (Mary Cuthbertson) was voted Most Valuable Player and received a spot on the all-tourney team at West Charlotte High in Charlotte, North Carolina. My fellow teammates were Mary Pryer, Erma Freeman, Willie Johnson, Victoria Miller, Kay Pryer, Emma Howie, Peggy Freeman, Lillian Kiser, Helena Howell, and Maxine Young. We took each game seriously and played as a team without complaining. The Logan boys' team did not place as winners in the tournament in 1956.

One unique thing about buses transporting students to Logan from across the county was the shortened school day when it rained. If it began to rain extremely hard in the morning and continued, an early closing announcement would be sent to each classroom. It meant that school would close at one in the afternoon to allow the buses to leave before the county roads became muddy or the water rose over small, narrow bridges. When the day was shortened due to rain, it was called teaching through, and it covered about four high school classes. The white students were sent home early also because they rode buses as well.

Many times, students both white and black would go to

the movies because the theaters opened at one o'clock. School administrators learned about students going to the theaters and stopped closing early for rain. I never went to the movies because most of the time I didn't have the money and I didn't want to walk in the rain to get there anyway.

Logan didn't have a cafeteria, so those of us who walked to school went home for lunch or to the stores near the school to purchase something if we had money. The students who rode the bus would bring lunch or go to the home economics classroom to buy soup and a sandwich or go to the stores. The principal allowed the home economics teacher to prepare food and sell it with the money being used to replenish the food supplies. A bowl of soup and crackers cost five cents, and there was a variety of menu items that changed during the week depending on how much time Katie E. Jones and her students had for preparation. The class that came to her for home economics after lunch washed the dishes.

The state school buses provided transportation for students who lived in Cabarrus County to attend Logan High and Shankletown Elementary as well as white students who attended white-only schools. In the morning, the elementary school students were unloaded at Shankletown and then at Logan. In the afternoon, it was the reverse with students being picked up last at Shankletown because the buses and the drivers were at Logan.

Our teachers and the principal lived in the community surrounding the two schools. They were members of the various churches and knew the students they were teaching and their parents in Concord. Therefore, it was easy to have an effect on our behavior since parents and teachers could be in contact any day of the week. It was a little harder to contact parents of students who lived farther out in the county except by sending a note with the students.

We were taught morals and values in addition to the regular subjects, and that boosted our self-confidence. Our teachers never allowed us to think of ourselves as less than white people. God had made us in his image, and we were bewildered by the thought that whites could believe differently. During discussions, the question always came up about why whites who believed in the Bible thought blacks were less human than they were.

In elementary school, we began the day by saluting the American flag, and then each student would recite a Bible verse. Between school and church, we would amass a number of Bible verses because it was embarrassing if we knew only one or two.

Our school sponsored numerous social activities. All grades from elementary to high school participated in May Day activities; dances and the wrapping of the May Pole dominated the program that day. Wrapping the pole looked easy when everyone concentrated on going in the correct order; that was why practice was so important. Once the pole was wrapped, it was unwrapped, and that required the same precision. May Day was coordinated by the physical education department with teachers on every grade level helping their students prepare for the big day. It wasn't celebrated every year, but when it was, we really enjoyed it.

Dances were held on Friday nights after football games. The games were played at Webb Field, which was behind Concord High. It was the only stadium in the city, and it exists to this day though it is not used for high school football games.

The Logan mascot was the tiger, and the colors were black and gold. Concord High's colors were the same with the spider as its mascot. After the court's decision to integrate schools, the one thing African Americans had left to identify with was the black and gold.

Logan's marching band under the direction Carl O. Foster was very good. It performed during halftime at football games at home and away as well as marching in the annual Christmas parade. The instruments the school owned were secondhand; we received them from Concord High. Others were bought by the students' parents. The majority of our schoolbooks were secondhand—we would always see one or two names already on the inside. When we got a book with only one name or by some strange circumstance a new book, we were extremely excited. However, we never let the fact that our books were hand-me-downs interfere with learning. Carl Foster was the choral director as well, and the chorus won numerous high ratings at choral competitions.

For many years, we looked forward to the Halloween Bazaar held in the gymnasium on the last Thursday and Friday nights of October. Each high school homeroom class would sponsor a booth. They were set up similar to those at the county fair and consisted of food and trinkets for sale, games, and space for dancing. The money went into the class treasuries. Collecting admissions at the door was handled by the junior or senior classes because they were responsible for the junior prom and senior yearbook. Those classes alternated each year so each could help defray the cost of the prom and the yearbook. When one of the nights actually fell on Halloween, we had fun seeing how inventive students could be dressing up in costumes. Many students came to the bazaar after trick-or-treating. For some reason, we didn't have a bazaar every year while I was in high school.

The football season included homecoming and the crowning of Miss Logan, the homecoming queen. At African American high schools, homecoming queen competition was a fundraiser to supplement the athletic program. The girl who raised the most money was crowned Miss Logan. Some years, we had a homecoming parade. Classes sponsored floats, which students decorated with their homeroom teachers' guidance. Teachers and students worked together to raise money for the materials and to design the floats. James Polk, who taught English, was also the senior class adviser and in charge of graduation. He allowed us to work on committees to plan the homecoming activities and supervised the presentation of a play each year.

For the homecoming parade, we went to car dealers and asked to use their convertibles, developed the parade route and lineup for parade day, and got permission from the city. The class advisers allowed their students to make major decisions because they believed it was a learning process the students would carry over into their adult lives. I look back on those years and realize we were fortunate to have had those experiences. I found myself using some of what I learned in high school throughout my career as a teacher and later as a guidance counselor.

Every year, the senior class was responsible for producing the yearbook. During my senior year, we produced the layout for the yearbook and started the first school newspaper. I was the first editor of *The Log* as it was named; we sold it for ten cents a copy. We had reporters who represented each high school homeroom and special reporters who gathered the elementary school news for each edition.

A senior class play helped reduce the cost of the yearbook; students and adults sold tickets to people in the community whether or not they had children in the senior class. Mr. Polk always made sure that the students in the play knew their parts and were well rehearsed.

The Logan girls' and boys' basketball teams were outstanding, but neither team won a championship during my four years as a player. Coaches and other teachers provided our transportation to tournaments, usually held in Charlotte. That meant we would eat at an African American restaurant. Our favorite was El Chico's. The name would suggest it was Mexican, but it was owned and operated by an African American family. They served the best home-cooked-style meals.

The principal gave our coaches enough to pay for our meals from the athletic budget; we students were told how much we could spend. On the way home from a night game, we sometimes stopped at a white restaurant that had curb service. We could order sandwiches and drinks, which we ate while sitting in our cars. The people who took the orders at these places were called carhops, and yes, most of them were white. We weren't allowed to go inside to eat in restaurants in the 1950s. We players paid for our food at the drive-in with our own money.

In later years, we had an activity bus for transportation and for out-of-town games. The girls' and boys' tournaments were scheduled for different dates so there wouldn't be any conflicts as far as transportation was concerned.

The longest distance we traveled to play basketball was to Asheville, North Carolina, to play Stevens Lee High. On that day, we left school before one o'clock in order to arrive early enough to eat a light meal and rest before the game. Mr. Banner always scheduled a stop at Chimney Rock, where there were shops and a telescope we could use to view the beautiful, breathtaking scenery.

Stevens Lee High was atop a steep side of a mountain. It was so steep that we had to get off the bus and walk up steep steps to reach the campus because the bus couldn't make it up to the campus with passengers on board.

After a light meal and a short rest, we would have a shoot-around in the gym before the game. Our teams never beat Stevens Lee in Concord or there. The joke was that we couldn't beat those mountaineers.

I learned that two kinds of milk were served in the cafeteria at Stevens Lee—goat and cow milk. I loved drinking milk, so when my teammates didn't want their milk, they gave it to me. One time, when I drank what I thought was regular milk, I noticed it tasted different and I thought it was spoiled. I told one of the Stevens Lee players who was helping serve us about the taste, and she told me it was goat milk. The next time we traveled there for a game, I made sure I was given cow's milk.

When the game was over and we were about to make the trip back home, we assembled again in the cafeteria for a light snack to keep us from getting hungry as we traveled home. We would get back to Concord at about half past midnight and have to go to school the next day since the trip was not on a Friday.

═══ CHAPTER 6 ═══

Insurance for
African Americans

Our parents and neighbors in our African American community were at the mercy of white people who got wealthy selling insurance that was available only through them until North Carolina Mutual Insurance Company was founded by Asa T. Spaulding.

White insurance companies sold black people insurance policies worth $200 or $500 that required payments of 10¢–25¢ that white agents collected every two weeks. Usually, there was no date given for when the policy would be paid up. Those companies took advantage of black people because they knew they didn't know how much they would pay for the face value of those policies.

Until I was seven or eight, I never saw any black person in our community who sold insurance and collected payments. North Carolina Mutual began offering insurance in higher amounts with affordable premiums, which helped black people get more for their money, and the company offered endowments for children to help pay for college education, something white insurance companies never mentioned. It was not their intent to help us or our parents realize college was an option.

Part of the money for my college tuition came from an endowment policy my mother purchased that Mr. Shuford, a North Carolina Mutual agent, sold her when he first began working in Concord. He didn't have a car, so he walked around town going from house to house explaining the different policies and helping people make choices. North Carolina Mutual became the largest African American insurance company in America and retained that status for many years.

Aetna Insurance insured slaves for plantation owners, and CSX insured slaves who built railroads and other businesses in America. The plantation owners collected the premiums when the black workers died. The white companies did not offer hospitalization insurance to families either. North Carolina Mutual offered the full gamut of policies to African Americans, and when they were financially able, they bought policies for their families.

CHAPTER 7

College Days

After graduating from Logan High in 1956, I enrolled at Barber-Scotia College as a day student to pursue a degree in education. There were few career choices for African Americans in the South before integration. Teachers were needed more than most other professionals were then. To earn money to help pay for college expenses, girls took domestic employment—cleaning the homes of white people, washing and ironing clothes, or babysitting their children during the summer. Many of the more wealthy white families would take an African American females with them to the beach or the mountains while they vacationed; the black females would care for the children and perform housekeeping chores. I never agreed to work for anyone who expected me to do that. Some college students would go north to such places as New Jersey, Washington, DC, or New York to work during the summer because the pay was better.

During the summer before my freshman year at Barber-Scotia College, I worked for a white couple who worked at Cannon Mills—the Cannon towel and sheet manufacturer.

I babysat their two school-aged boys and did the cleaning, laundry, and cooking for three months. I never mentioned that I would be working only until classes started at college. White people didn't like the idea of black people going to college, so when we applied for jobs, we never let them know we were college students.

I did give one week's notice that I would be leaving, and on my last day, I told them I would be entering college. Our older college friends told us younger ones that we should never let anyone know our intentions. If they asked, we would lie and say no because we knew we would be working somewhere else the next summer. There was no financial aid or grants and only a few scholarships to pay for college those years. Work-study aid went to students living on campus. Many students could not enroll in college even though they were scholastically eligible because their families did not have the money. My husband, Benjamin, fell into that category and did not get the chance to further his education though he was academically eligible.

Many students whose parents were buying a home could use it as collateral for a loan for tuition, but my mother was a renter. Nonetheless, she was able to get one of my elementary school teachers and his wife to cosign for a loan. She never missed a payment. The president of Concord National Bank (now Fifth Third Bank) knew her because she worked at the dry cleaners downtown. He would always say when he spoke to her that she had never missed a payment.

During my freshman year, my next-door neighbor told me about an opening at Colonial Motor Court, the motel where she worked, as a weekend cleaner. I applied and was hired. That meant I would be working on weekends and would miss church. I worked there for a year on weekends through the academic year and all week during the summer from fall 1956 until September 1957.

When the women who worked full-time were off for whatever reason, they needed someone to work in their places, which gave me the opportunity to make more money. My mother told me it would be a big help to her if I bought some of my clothes, so I developed a plan for getting the most for my money. I saved money all summer, spending only what I had to, and then shopped for the clothing needed for the school year in September.

My mother worked two jobs to provide the necessities for normal living and pay the loan for my tuition and fees. Looking back at the way she had to juggle paying the rent one week, the utilities the next, buying groceries and clothing, and then making the loan payments, I realize she was the first financial planner I ever knew. No one was using that terminology during the 1950s and 1960s. I learned early how to be keep track of expenditures by writing them down and comparing income to outgo, which today is called a spending plan.

My mother (Sallie) taught me how to sew during the summer before my freshman year in high school. I had watched her make dresses, skirts, and suits for both of us from early childhood. We were very adept at making our clothing, so nearly half of our clothes were handmade. The one thing we always kept in mind was that the clothing we made had to look as if we had bought it rather than made it even if it meant ripping out and putting the garment together again. I learned to extend my wardrobe by mixing the old with the new whether I had bought or made them. We never sewed for other people because we didn't have time. Besides, potential customers didn't understand how much time it took to make a garment.

By the time I reached college, my sewing skills were really developed and I could look at fabric and imagine how it would look as a garment. I went downtown one day after class at Barber-Scotia and bought a yard of wool cloth that was fifty-four inches wide, a zipper, thread, a half yard of lining, and hem tape. After dinner that night, I placed the pattern pieces on the fabric for the skirt, cut the pieces, and began stitching I completed it later in the week. Of course that happened to be a night that I didn't have homework or an early morning class. Being creative produced the uniqueness I liked.

I continued making clothing when I started teaching; I made half of my wardrobe. Teachers' pay was not that high, so rather than buying everything off the rack in stores, I mixed and matched my clothes as I had done in college. Besides, sewing was an excellent way to relieve stress after being with students all day. Most of the people couldn't tell whether the clothing my mother and I wore had been bought or was handmade. The key was to choose quality fabrics on sale and work to achieve perfection when putting the garment together.

Barber-Scotia College provided me the same kind of nurturing that Logan High had. We were encouraged not only to learn but also to value ourselves as competent individuals. The college strongly emphasized how important it was to perfect our educational skills so we could compete with our white counterparts when that day came.

The faculty was integrated in the 1950s and 1960s before the courts declared segregation unconstitutional. Barber-Scotia had begun as Scotia Seminary in 1866; it was established by the Presbyterian Church (USA) along with Westminster Presbyterian Church and Rev. Luke Dorland, a white missionary who came to Cabarrus County from Toledo, Ohio.

The seminary was established to educate young black women of the South. Dr. Leland S. Cozart served as the first African American president from 1937 until his retirement in 1967. All other presidents before him were white ministers as well. Dr. Cozart was the first president who wasn't a minister. He was a very stern administrator who projected high standards for us. We were taught to be young ladies with high morals, pride, and self-confidence. The male students were taught to respect young ladies at all times as well as themselves and to be strong, confident men.

Because Barber-Scotia was a Presbyterian school, it was easy to see why attracting white instructors was normal. There were full- and part-time white faculty members who never exhibited any subtle or blatant prejudice toward students. Achievement expectations were high in the classroom regardless of the instructor's race.

Dr. Susan Shock was a white English instructor who was employed full-time. She was as comfortable on campus as any African American faculty member was. She was an excellent teacher—strict and hard but willing to help students reach their potential. She lived on the campus, and I admired and respected her dedication. She had not married because she told us her fiancé had been killed in an accident, and so she was dedicated to teaching.

White faculty members could live on or off campus. The part-time faculty members commuted from Davidson College, Davidson, Charlotte, or Salisbury, North Carolina.

Having white instructors gave us an opportunity to learn that all whites did not want to keep us illiterate. We students didn't have any way of knowing whether other private colleges had white instructors. The two private colleges closest to Concord were Johnson C. Smith in Charlotte and Livingstone College in Salisbury, North Carolina. Because we always had white instructors, we accepted that as normal and learned as much as we could in their classes just as we did in classes taught by African American instructors.

Even at Logan High, the part-time Bible teacher was white. In addition to the white instructors at Barber-Scotia, we also had a Chinese home economics instructor who lived on campus. Barber-Scotia was multicultural long before the word was used extensively. The school became coed and multicultural all in the same era. The first white male student enrolled in 1953. The next year, African American males enrolled. Many of them were veterans who were taking advantage of the GI Bill (the generic term comprising various education assistance programs administered by the Department of Veterans Affairs).

It was said that the first African American males were told by President Cozart that they were to open doors for young ladies and let them enter the building before them even if they were several feet away from the doors. That was before I was enrolled as a student.

═══ CHAPTER 8 ═══

The Beginning of the Quest for Equal Rights

The first sit-ins ignited protest marches and boycotting of stores throughout the South by African Americans. After the lunch counter sit-ins began in February 1960 in Greensboro, North Carolina, students at Barber-Scotia went to Belk Department Store in downtown Concord and sat at the snack bar. They were not served, and the police were called. In Concord, Belk store manager Ray Cline immediately had a wall built around the lunch counter, which was in the store's basement. White patrons had to enter through a door. The two African American women who worked there cleaning and running the elevator could no longer buy anything there to take with them as had been the policy.

I was a senior at Barber-Scotia and was away from campus for student teaching at Logan High when the sit-ins began, as were other of my classmates. When we returned to the campus and attempted to join the protest marches, the organizers would not allow us to do so. It was never explained why, but we seniors felt they were trying to protect us because we would soon be in the market for jobs.

The marches continued from February until the end of the school year. African Americans refused to purchase merchandise from Belk; those who had charge accounts there closed them. Many, like my mother, never opened an account there again. To this day, I don't have a Belk charge card. Belk was the only store with a visible ladies' lounge, but it was for white only. We had to be prepared for not needing to use the restroom when we went out shopping. However, if the need became urgent, we would go to the bus station, which was near the stores, or we could walk around to Church Street to use the colored restroom.

During the years colored and white restrooms and water fountains were prevalent, we would drink from both when no one was looking. We would laugh as we turned them on; the water was the same, so we wondered what the difference was.

The college students who marched relentlessly in front of the Belk store daily were spit on and called names, and several were arrested, but that did not make them stop the nonviolent protest against the segregation we endured. The local chapter of the NAACP posted bail and provided legal help through the state NAACP.

Lunch counter sit-ins spread across the South, and a good number of legal cases made their way to the courts for the desegregation of public eateries. The courts decided after many months that it was time to end another form of segregation. The wall around the lunch counter came down at Belk, and the ladies' lounge was opened to both races after the court's decision.

Before the bus boycott in Birmingham, Alabama, African

Americans rode in the back of the bus though they paid the same fare as whites did. Such buses provided transportation in Concord and Kannapolis, North Carolina. I often tried my luck when riding them by not going to the back if there were just a few passengers. I would go about halfway and sit down in the last seat across from the side door at the back of the bus and watch as the driver and passengers looked at me. I wasn't asked to move.

The thousands of African Americans who had moved north for better jobs took trains and buses back home for vacations and holidays. Once southbound trains left Washington, DC, African Americans were allowed to occupy only one or two cars. When all the seats were filled, they had to stand until passengers departed at stops. Another passenger car would be added in Salisbury, North Carolina, when overcrowding occurred in either direction, north or south, and supplies would be added as well. That meant the stop in Salisbury would take longer than others did. I observed the overcrowding when my relatives were boarding the train to return north after visiting in Concord on vacation. Sometimes, the cars were so crowded that they would have to wait for the next train, and that happened especially in the summer. As the train arrived, we would see empty seats in the white-only cars.

My mother and I traveled by train to Washington, DC, to see Grandpa James Cuthbertson. As the train was approaching Salisbury, the conductor announced that the stop there would be a little long because supplies were being loaded. We looked out and saw ice and food being loaded. Of course, we could not eat in the dining car until the train passed north of the Mason-Dixon line. During the days of segregated transportation, African Americans had to take food with them when traveling on trains or buses not only because of segregation but also because most could not afford to eat in the dining car. When buses stopped at the bus stations along the route, passengers again were separated by having to go to white-only and colored-only waiting areas and restrooms.

When the Birmingham, Alabama, bus boycott court decision struck down segregation, interstate and intrastate laws were implemented. The law was hard to enforce because it was not easy for many to understand. The judges didn't say all transportation was to begin becoming integrated; that was an easy out for them. Dual waiting rooms still existed at many bus and train stations. One Friday, Josephine, a college classmate, and I decided to go to Charlotte to shop after classes that day. Many male students at Scotia were veterans who had second-shift jobs to supplement their GI benefits, and Elzavan Plunkett was one of them. We asked him to take us downtown; we planned to take the bus back to Concord. The stores stayed open until nine o'clock on Friday night. I didn't think about leaving a note for my mother to let her know where I was going when I went home for lunch. When I didn't get home at usual time, she was worried because she didn't know where I was. We returned home just before eight thirty, and once she heard the story, her worry was for good reason.

Having never been to the bus station before, Josephine and I entered the first door we came to, which placed us in the white waiting room. We purchased our tickets and noticed the strange looks we got from whites. Through a window behind the person selling tickets, we saw African Americans peering at us from the other side. The white folks didn't know what to do, and Josephine and I were both light skinned, so I suppose that helped. We realized we were on the wrong side, but we decided not to change; we sat to wait for the bus. The wait was a little longer than we'd anticipated, so Josephine and I walked to a newsstand to buy snacks.

We took the bus back to Concord, got off near Barber-Scotia on Corban Avenue, and walked home. We lived in opposite directions, but there wasn't any fear of walking alone at night, because there was no fear of being harmed by anyone. As more African Americans challenged the intrastate and interstate court rulings, the barriers slowly began falling. Integration of passenger seating became a reality.

═══ CHAPTER 9 ═══

The First Black Political Candidates

Shortly after the 1965 Voter Rights Act was passed, we as a people could not be denied the right to vote. Mr. A. T. Cordery was the finance director at Barber-Scotia, and his wife, Dr. Sara Cordery, was a professor there. Mr. Cordery was well known for his work at the college, and he was also well known in Presbyterian Church circles locally and nationally.

He filed to run for alderman in Concord's Ward Four, which was all black; he most likely would have won the election, but to thwart his win, some white person or persons looked around the ward searching for another black candidate to run against him.

Rev. Lowery was well known because he and his family owned and operated a store where many people in the community shopped for food. Someone convinced him to run and supposedly financed his campaign. He held rallies and served an abundance of barbecue and hot dogs with all the trimmings free to all who attended. Neither candidate won, because the black vote was split between the two black men, so the white candidate won as was planned.

Before the next election, Ward Four's boundaries were changed to include white people; instead of just one precinct, there were two. The change ensured the election of a white person because a black person could not be elected without white votes.

Before the 1965 Voter Rights Act, few black people voted. Black people had to pay a poll tax to be eligible to vote. White candidates knew that only a small number of blacks voted, and they used that to their advantage. They would make visits in the communities to introduce themselves and give monetary gifts to self-proclaimed community leaders for the black vote. Everyone who understood the political process knew it was an act of tokenism because white candidates could win with or without the black vote.

In 1979, Mr. Robert L. Mathis became the first black person to win a seat as an alderman in Concord representing Ward Four, and he served for seventeen years. There are still two precincts, one predominately black the other predominately white. When Concord decided to change from wards to districts, Ward Four became District Three and expanded because of increased population.

I have referenced this incident not only as a matter of history but also to demonstrate that boundaries have always been drawn to thwart the election of blacks and that the courts have never ruled unconstitutional districts that ensured the majority was white. However, when the Twelfth Congressional District in North Carolina was drawn with the majority being black, ensuring the election of the same, that was challenged more than once in the courts. Historically, all district boundaries were drawn to benefit white voters for control. There is still to this day prejudice toward black politicians by whites who still feel blacks are inferior and are not intelligent enough to represent them.

On November 4, 2008, Barack Obama, a Democrat, became the first African American president of the United States; Americans of all races and ethnic backgrounds had felt the need for a change from eight years of Republican leadership.

I never understood why whites thought blacks didn't have some degree of intelligence and reasoning. We learned to survive white oppression by studying them. Even illiterate slaves learned to outsmart their masters by developing the skills necessary to ease the workloads and plan escapes to freedom. Though many did not succeed in running away, they demonstrated that slaves were intelligent enough to follow the directions of those who planned their escapes.

After the 2000 census, North Carolina gained another US congressional seat, making it necessary to redraw district boundaries. The North Carolina legislature drew new boundaries, but they were challenged in court as being too favorable toward Democrats and had to be redrawn. Judge Knox Jenkins chose to draw the boundaries himself. The North Carolina legislature filed an appeal with the Supreme Court. The judges would not overturn the lower court judge's ruling, so the new district boundaries favoring Republicans became final. The judge who drew the boundaries was a Republican appointee.

The 2002 election was delayed for lack of agreement about whether the new boundary lines should remain as drawn or be changed. By the time it was determined that no changes would be made and the election could proceed, there was little time left for campaigning. Many politicians, judges, and some voters are still not happy with the Twelfth Congressional District's boundaries and continue to file motions in court for change, but it remains the same.

≡ CHAPTER 10 ≡

Job Market Changes

Today's numerous house and commercial cleaning services are owned and staffed by whites and blacks. At one time, black women could not work at Cannon Mills, the historical giant sheet and towel manufacturer, as anything other than custodians. It was the same at Kerr Bleachery, which manufactured fabrics in Concord. There were hosiery mills as well, but they too did not hire black women in production.

When President John F. Kennedy's administration began to put pressure on companies through the Justice Department and the courts eventually struck down discrimination in hiring, it became unconstitutional to deny employment strictly because of color.

Prior to the Kennedy era, black women were employed in laundries, in dry cleaners as pressers, or in hospitals, clothing stores, and furniture stores as custodians and domestic workers. A few clothing stores and dry cleaners employed black women for alterations if they had excellent sewing skills. Black men were relegated to custodial jobs at banks and other business that paid less than what white men earned in the mills. Black men who worked in the mills could load and unload trucks with merchandise and keep the loading areas clean. Likewise, they could open the bales of cotton for processing for spinning fabric to make sheets and towels.

There were no black male supervisors before the law forbidding discrimination in hiring took effect. However, many of the white supervisors had less education than some of the black employees. At the post office, black males were custodians. Since that was a federal job, the pay was higher than at other places. For many years, black communities did not have mail delivered to houses, so black people had to go to the post office and ask for their mail. There was a white person, usually female, who sat at the window with a wall behind her that had alphabetical mail slots. We would say our name and address, and she would retrieve our mail and hand it to us.

Once house-to-house delivery began in black neighborhoods, the mail carriers were all white males. Some were very friendly, but others were not. All mail clerks were white; their job was to sort the mail for the mail slots in the mail rooms and outgoing mail. Young black men did not have the desire to be janitors because of the stigma associated with that unless there were absolutely no other jobs available. That is why so many young adults left the South to pursue better paying jobs. Even then, some ended up with the same kind of job, but they earned more in the North.

Numerous trucking companies that delivered products nationwide were in Charlotte. Many black males, especially those who had served in the armed forces, were able to get jobs loading and unloading trucks.

Black people have always marveled at the naïveté of whites

who trusted their children and cooking to black maids. The majority of the whites thought blacks were prone to thievery, stupid, and less than human. However, the maids developed very good relationships with their children. The hours were sometimes long for those who worked for Miss Ann and Mr. Charlie, our nicknames for whomever the family happened to be. We as a people cooked the meals for white families who ate them without reservations and loved it. However, it never occurred to them that something could be put in their food. We saw what Kizzie did when she spit in the glass of water that she gave to the white girl she had grown up with on the plantation as depicted in the television movie *Roots*. However, I never heard that anyone did that while working in the homes of any white families.

The majority of white families were generous with leftover food; the maids could take some of it home to their families. Sometimes, mean and stingy whites would allow their maids only one meal during the workday. The black maid was usually away from her own home all day and would have to do the same thing for her family that she had done during the day after she got home. A familiar sight in white communities was a black woman pushing a stroller or carriage or walking with older children along sidewalks.

During summer, some families would take their maids to the beach or the mountains when they vacationed; that meant the maids had to leave their families so they could keep their jobs. The same kind of work paid more up north than it did in the South, so many young females moved there. They either lived with the families ("on the lot," as it was termed) or with relatives who had migrated north and had living quarters. The best deal was living on the lot because the living quarters, food, and utilities were provided making it possible to save money. The only drawback was being so isolated and not having anyone to talk to. Sometimes, there were opportunities to talk with other maids while on outings with the children they were caring for.

During the days before equal employment opportunities, blacks who were employed in the homes of whites were tested. The white women would leave money and jewelry lying around to see if their colored girls, as they were called, would take it. To find out if she had done a thorough job cleaning, Miss Ann would run her hands over the furniture to see if it had been dusted underneath objects. She would look under sofas and beds to check for dust. Some were very kind to their domestic help, but many were not. Those not so nice would demand that their sheets and underwear be ironed. The time for leaving could be late depending on when dinner was and the time it took the maid to clean up. Many white families would give their colored "girls" Christmas gifts that would benefit their families.

After the court decision struck down discrimination in hiring, black women could apply for other kinds of employment, thus reducing the number of domestic workers available in the South. Those black women who continued as domestic workers and babysitters could demand more money.

Today, there is a no stigma associated with cleaning homes for whites because it has become a business. The doors were opened for cleaning services both residential and commercial because finding people to work full-time was next to impossible. Now, women of both races have cleaning businesses that allow them to work for themselves.

CHAPTER 11

Breaking the Barriers of Segregation

Lawrence C. Evans Sr. was the first African American to be hired as a police officer in the mid-1950s. He walked his beat in the black community because he was not given a patrol car. A phone was set up on his beat so Officer Evans could call the police department to ask for a white officer to come and pick up someone he had arrested.

Later, other officers were employed in the late fifties and sixties including David "Chalk" Steele Sr., Charles Pless Sr., William Boger Sr., Sylvester Steele, and Julius Franklin. Franklin became the first black detective with the Concord Police Department. Before integration, however, black officers could not patrol anywhere except in black neighborhoods.

When the Christmas parade was held in downtown Concord, the black officers could not help patrol the crowd; only white officers did that. Black people could not gather and mix with the whites at the parade. Slowly, as integration began, black officers were allowed to begin patrolling at the parades but just in the area where black people were standing.

In the beginning of the 1970s, black officers were no longer required to segregate themselves at the parades, and neither were black attendees.

In 1971, Clarence Lawing became the first black fireman hired by the Concord Fire Department. In later years, he was promoted and became the first black captain. In 1972, Steve Shipp was hired, and he too was promoted during his career with the department and became the first black battalion chief.

Trucking companies began hiring black males to drive their trucks long distance; that had not been the case until then. My husband, Benjamin, was among the first group hired to work for Johnson Motor Lines in Charlotte; he went to North Carolina State University for training. The black males who had been working on the loading docks were grandfathered into driving positions without training.

The first African American attorney was Marnite Shuford Perry, who practiced with the late James Johnson in 1975 in Concord. After a short period, Marnite moved her practice to Charlotte. She spent her early childhood in Concord before her father died. Mr. Shuford (I have not been able to learn his first name) was employed by North Carolina Mutual Insurance Company.

Vernon A. Russell became the first African American male attorney in 1981 and is a partner in the Plummer Russell Plummer law firm. Betty E. Eddleman was the first to be elected as a member of the Concord City Schools Board of Education. Betty B. Alston served as a member of Cabarrus County Board of Education. The Concord City School

System merged with Cabarrus County School System in 1983. Elaine P. Archie began her duties as the first Cabarrus County Magistrate in 1983 and retired in 2013. Robert M. Freeman (R) was appointed to fill a vacant seat on the Cabarrus County Board of Commissioners. He ran in an election to keep his seat and won; he served a full term but was defeated during the second campaign.

The first African American football player to be drafted to play with a national football team from Cabarrus County was Haskell Stanback, who played for the Atlanta Falcons. He was a graduate of A. L. Brown High School in Kannapolis, North Carolina. He received a scholarship to play football at the University of Tennessee.

Cabarrus Bank had branches in Kannapolis and Concord and was owned by Cannon Mills. The first African American to be employed as a teller was Laura Ruth McCullough at the Kannapolis bank. Before that, a bank owned by North Carolina Mutual Insurance Company was established in Durham, North Carolina—the Mechanics and Farmers Bank. Before integration began, the company decided to establish another bank in Charlotte. However, since that was a black-owned bank, anyone who was hired to work there was not integrating the staff because it was already all black.

CHAPTER 12

The Beginning of My Teaching Career

I began my career at Carver High School in Kannapolis at the beginning of the 1961/62 school year; I taught seventh- and eighth-grade science. Schools containing grades one through twelve were called union schools. The prior year, I had been a regular substitute teacher because I had not gotten a job near home. I wasn't exactly a new teacher, so during our first faculty meeting, Mr. William L. Reid, our principal, was reminded that he had forgotten to introduce me along with the other new teachers.

The veteran teachers provided as much mentoring for us as we needed without criticizing us; we definitely appreciated that and learned from them. Carver was still an all-black school though the Supreme Court had decided in the 1954 *Brown v. Board of Education* decision that separate but equal was unconstitutional.

Integrating schools across the South was a very slow process. The first option was the Freedom of Choice plan that allowed parents to enroll children in all-white schools as a way of getting around the court order. Everyone remembers seeing pictures of children being accompanied by police as they went to white schools to enroll. However, that kind of spectacle did not happen everywhere. After seeing television broadcasts of those disturbing incidents of resistance across the South, smaller school districts accepted the inevitable, and no police were needed.

The Freedom of Choice plan was put in place to allow black parents to enroll their children in white schools in any grade. Many parents were uneasy about allowing children to enter a school alone at the beginning. Soon, some parents felt someone had to be first to do that.

From 1964 through 1966, the Freedom of Choice plan allowed a small number of black students to enroll in white schools in Concord, Kannapolis, Charlotte, and other areas across the South. In Concord, a cross was burned in the yard of a black family that had enrolled one of their children in a white school, and there were some fires and destruction in Charlotte. Attorney Julius Chambers's office suffered because he had filed lawsuits against the Charlotte-Mecklenburg School System for not following the court order.

Also during this time, teachers were asked to leave segregated schools and go to all-white schools in a secretive way. The superintendent of the school system and the principal of the white school would decide on the placement of a black teacher in a subject or grade level that was vacant. Then the principal at the black school would be told of the need so that a black teacher could be chosen and notified of the change in school assignment. The faculty of the black school would not find out who was leaving until all the plans had been made.

The southern states thought the Freedom of Choice plan would satisfy the Department of Health, Education, and Welfare for many years, but it didn't. Another mandate was handed down by the court that all schools were to integrate with all due haste.

The enactment of the 1964 Civil Rights Act in response to the nonviolent civil rights movement finally spurred action. In 1966, in the *United States v. Jefferson County Board of Education*, the Fifth Circuit Court ordered school districts not only to end segregation but also to "undo the harm" segregation had caused by racially balancing their schools under federal guidelines.

That was followed by the Supreme Court's decision in 1968 that required desegregation right away. A strong federal commitment to the enforcement of the Civil Rights Act of 1964 proved to be critical. In the first five years after the act's passage, with the federal government threatening to and sometimes cutting federal funding to school districts that failed to comply with the law, more-substantial progress was made toward desegregating schools than had been made in the ten years following the Brown decision.

In 1964, only 1 percent of African American students in the South attended schools with whites. By 1966, the figure had risen to 3.2 percent. By the 1970s, according to studies by Gary Orfield, the South had become the nation's most integrated region. In 1976, 45.1 percent of the South's African American students were attending majority white schools compared with just 27.5 percent in the Northeast and 29.7 percent in the Midwest. These gains occurred in the context of the second great controversy of the school desegregation effort—busing.

The controversy came to a head in the Supreme Court's 1971 decision *Swann v. Charlotte-Mecklenburg Board of Education*, one of the first attempts to implement a large-scale urban desegregation plan. Swann called for district-wide desegregation and allowed the use of busing to achieve integration; it found that the times and distances involved in the desegregation plan were no more onerous that those meant to segregate students. Court-ordered busing, as it came to be known, was fiercely attacked and not the least by President Richard Nixon's administration.

Busing was criticized as undermining the sanctity of neighborhood schools; it was considered impractical, unworkable, intrusive, and inappropriate social engineering. While white busing drew a great deal of public attention, critics largely overlooked the facts that few students were bused for the purpose of desegregation and indeed that busing worked especially in the South, where school districts were often countywide and included cities and suburbs alike.

All schools had to begin integrating across the nation, but the South was hit hard from 1965 through 1968. White parents put pressure on school administrators not to assign their children to schools in black communities. Therefore, the majority of black schools were closed and the majority of their students and teachers were assigned to white schools. The percentage of black students and teachers had to be reported to the Department of Health, Education, and Welfare every year to meet federal guidelines. Each state had to keep the same records sent to HEW so they would keep the percentages up to par.

When a black teacher left a school, he or she had to be replaced with someone of the same race to keep the racial balance. Students were bused across districts to meet the racial requirements. Black students were traveling farther from home than were white students. Again, black students were the victims of busing. New districts or zones for school systems continued to be drawn for nearly twenty years to be sure there was a racial balance.

The Concord City Schools Board of Education authorized the building of a new high school on Burrage Road to replace the original Concord High, but that location was beyond walking distance for the black students at Logan High.

Concord is a municipality in Cabarrus County; there were two school districts—Concord City Schools and Cabarrus County Schools—until 1983, when the two consolidated and became the Cabarrus County School System. A group of black parents filed a lawsuit against the Concord School Board asking that black children be allowed to attend the new Concord High School. Three weeks before school was to begin in 1968, the judge presiding over the lawsuit issued the mandate that the new Concord High School would open as an integrated school or not at all. All the schedules and teacher assignments had to be changed within three weeks. There weren't enough buses to provide transportation, so the parents of the black students formed car pools. That first year worked more smoothly than anyone thought it would.

Before desegregation, there were only two high schools in the Concord School District—Concord and Logan. In the Cabarrus County District, there were four high schools—Mt. Pleasant, Bethel, Central Cabarrus, and Northwest Cabarrus. The court decision forced all the county schools to integrate as well. There were several elementary schools for white students but only two for black students. Logan High had grades one through twelve, and Shankletown Elementary had grades one through eight and was part of Cabarrus County School System.

Logan became an elementary school until it closed in 1970. The black students were assigned to McAllister, Coltrane Webb, Beverly Hills, and Clara Harris Elementary Schools. Black students were bused to those schools to meet desegregation requirements. The old Concord High became a junior high and remained that way for several years until the new concept of elementary, middle, and high schools emerged.

White parents did not want their children attending schools in black communities, so Logan High was demolished after closing in 1970. The gymnasium and the cafeteria were left standing, and the gymnasium became a recreation center as part of the Concord Recreation Department.

Several years later, Logan Daycare bought the cafeteria along with the vacant property and built a new facility there, and the daycare remains. The vacant property was used to build Logan Villas, low-income and senior housing.

In Kannapolis, the school board decided to keep Carver High open, and it became the seventh-grade center. In the late 1970s, the Kannapolis City School Board began the process of building a new school to replace the Carver Center. The first decision was to build two schools—one on the east side of the city and the other on the west; that would have meant that neither school would be in the predominately black community. However, residents in the black community protested and began to collect information concerning the number of acres needed to build a school on the same street where Carver was. North Carolina had guidelines for the number of acres needed for each grade level of schools. Once black citizens presented that information to the school board, its members could no longer declare there wasn't enough land to build the new school on the adjoining property.

Thus, the new Kannapolis Middle School was built on East C Street and opened for the 1981/82 school year. The name has been changed now to Kannapolis Intermediate School after a new middle school was built.

Before the new middle school was completed in 1981, many white parents did not embrace the idea of their children attending the Carver Seventh Grade Center as it had become known. It was on the fringe of the black community and had a black principal. A. L. Brown High School and the superintendent's office could be seen from the Carver Seventh Grade Center separated by East First Street. Those white parents enrolled their children in Concord at the private Cabarrus Academy on North Union Street for their seventh grade. These students were then transferred back to Kannapolis and enrolled in Cannon Junior High for grades eight and nine, and they finished high school at A. L. Brown. The grades were divided into one through six, the seventh-grade center, junior high—eight through nine—and high school—tenth through twelfth grades.

A white teacher who lived in Kannapolis and taught at Concord High School enrolled her child in Cabarrus Academy until she entered Concord High and subsequently graduated. In order to have a legal address for attendance at the high school, the mother rented an apartment near the school that they occupied during the week. Many private schools popped up in anticipation of integrating schools in the 1960s to provide alternatives to integrated public schools. Northside Baptist Church in Charlotte was one of the largest and best known. Buses from Northside Christian School traveled to Cabarrus and Rowan to pick up students. Charlotte Catholic School was operating as well, but I never saw any buses from that school or any others from private schools in this county.

═══ CHAPTER 13 ═══

Integration of Schools

When the court issued the mandate that schools would integrate with all due haste, I was ready. After all, we had been preparing for this all our lives. However, then as now, the white administrators and data compilers always perpetuated a gap in achievement between whites and blacks.

Black teachers knew we had a lot to prove as we began the next step in our careers. Numerous factors contribute to the low achievement of black students including low expectations for these students and failure by some (not all) white teachers to set high goals for black students and the subtle push necessary for them to succeed.

Black students were strongly encouraged to achieve in the segregated schools by their teachers and parents. The students set goals for themselves as well because they knew achieving them was expected of them. Because slaves had been denied access to learning for three hundred years, there was a special emphasis placed on education. A small number of blacks didn't complete their education or learn to read and write, but they always made education a priority for their children.

Because of economic conditions, many blacks had to drop out of school to work and support their families. However, black people did not know that whites dropped out of school to go to work as well and that many could not read or write either.

J. W. Bullock, the superintendent of Kannapolis City Schools at that time, accepted the mandate of the court and the state to make integration as smooth as possible, but that did not mean all whites were pleased with the idea of blacks and whites together in school.

Now that schools were going to become integrated, black parents placed an even greater emphasis on achievement and continued to support their children in their new educational settings. They knew their children's performance would be scrutinized more than ever.

I began teaching at Cannon Junior High—grades eight and nine—at the beginning of the 1967/68 school year, and the principal was Daniel Hamrick Sr. My assigned subject was earth science and health. Science teachers rather than physical education teachers were assigned health classes for several years, but we were not told why. We taught health classes one day a week. The student load for teachers at junior highs and high schools was five classes per day that did not exceed 150 students. Teachers were assigned to monitor a study hall for one period per day. Eventually, study hall was eliminated by assigning students more classes. Our principal had extra duties for teachers whom he felt could help with disciplinary referrals from teachers. He appointed two female and two male teachers for that duty and included an hour per day to accomplish the task. The title was Dean of Girls and Dean of Boys with the students assigned by dividing the alphabet in half between the teachers. I was assigned the first half of the girls' alphabet; however, teachers could place their referrals in the mailbox of the teacher of their choice. We were given guidelines for discipline just as if we were assistant principals. After resolving problems, we gave the principal, Daniel Hamrick Sr., copies of the referrals for his approval. He then would take them to the superintendent's office to be filed.

Our integrated faculty and staff at Cannon Junior High (from 1967 to 1981, when it closed), became a very caring group. We experienced the same kind of camaraderie at G. W. Carver High and later at Kannapolis Middle School. When there was illness, death, or other problems, we helped each other as much as we could.

There were fun times as well. At Carver, William L. Reid would have a meal prepared for the faculty and served in the cafeteria on the day school was closing for the Christmas holidays. He would tell us to dress up. He also made sure there was enough food so we could take home some for our families as well. We could also play Secret Santa with our fellow faculty members and give and receive gifts at the dinner as well.

At Cannon Junior High, the student council members and their adviser would prepare a brunch for faculty and staff on the first day of school or on one of the workdays. We played Secret Santa for a week and set limits on the final gifts and daily ones as well. Sometimes, teachers would deliver gifts to other teachers, or put them in mailboxes, or perhaps send them through a student. The final gift was received during a short faculty meeting prior to closing for the holiday, and we would be completely surprised.

Faculty members arranged for an assortment of snacks in the teachers' lounge each day of the week before school closed for Christmas. We could choose something to eat during the planning period or at lunch. Our principal, Daniel Hamrick Sr., would have snacks in his office on the last day for teachers and staff and invite the superintendent to come to our school.

Our students went to their homerooms to enjoy snacks and listen to music during the last two periods. At Kannapolis Middle School, where the principal was Milton Taylor, we followed a similar procedure on the last day. There, teachers and staff members who did not have classes would relieve the homeroom teachers so they could go to the lounge for treats while their students enjoyed snacks and music.

I don't mean to make it seem as though we were not working. As a faculty, we set high goals for our students, and we used every technique at our disposal to help them reach those goals. However, the times spent together without students enabled us to learn our strengths in our subject areas as we worked together for greater proficiency.

On days when students were not in attendance, we worked on report cards and lesson plans for the next grading period. The students were eager to learn, and we had the support of their parents, so we used every method we could to help them reach their potential.

Those were the good old days of teaching. Of course there were discipline problems, some of which were just teenagers being teenagers, but nothing like there are today in our schools. The students accepted and showed respect for African American teachers just as much as they did their white counterparts, and that made our jobs easier.

═══ CHAPTER 14 ═══

Marriage and Family

After beginning my career in teaching at George Washington Carver High, I met a gentleman, Benjamin Blakeney, and we began dating. He unfortunately did not have the financial support from his family to go to college as was the case with many other capable individuals.

He went to work for Cannon Mills and was a singer with group known as the El Roccos. He worked during the week at the mill and traveled with the group on weekends to perform at African American colleges. Many of their trips required them to travel out of North Carolina. Because of segregation, accommodations were limited and the trips were very tiresome. In 1965, Benjamin was drafted into the army and spent a year in South Korea; he trained to set up telephone communication lines.

He returned from Korea in 1966, and we were married before his departure to Colorado to complete his service and receive his discharge in 1967. That was a time of employment changes brought about by federal law, but there was resistance to the law that race could no longer be used to deny employment. When Benjamin applied for employment at the Concord Telephone Company (now Windstream) as a lineman, he was not hired.

He was hired at Cannon Mills to load trucks that delivered textile products to other mills. After a short time, he became a truck driver and delivered products to other Cannon plants in Cabarrus and Rowan Counties. Previously, all truck drivers had been white and the loaders had been black. They would move the trucks in and out of the bays for loading and unloading.

Wanting something more, Benjamin applied for a position with North Carolina Mutual Life Insurance Company as an agent, and he was hired. During this time, we became the proud parents of our son, Daman, a source of joy and pride. Because we were both working, we placed our son in Logan Daycare. After two years, we enrolled Daman in Barber-Scotia College's Kiddie College for preschool and daycare. The children were in preschool in the morning with certified teachers and daycare for the remainder of the day. Children at the Kiddie College were definitely prepared for first grade at age six because of preschool.

Benjamin stayed with the insurance company for three years until the large trucking companies began hiring black drivers. Benjamin applied at Johnson Motor Lines in Charlotte and was hired. He enrolled in driver training at North Carolina State University in Raleigh to receive his commercial driver's license. He remained with the company until it went out of business.

He joined the Harold Goodman American Legion Post 172 and eventually became the post commander. After several years, he was elected commander of District Seventeen. He also became the chartered president of the Logan Optimists' Club with forty-six members, which was believed to have been a record at that time.

I began classes at the University of North Carolina at Charlotte to pursue a master's degree in guidance and counseling. During the 1975/76 school year, a guidance counselor position was available, and I was given the opportunity to change from teacher to guidance counselor.

Daman became a member of the Cabarrus County Boys Club (now the Cabarrus Boys and Girls Club) and participated in activities there. We enjoyed watching the little boys play football, baseball, and basketball. In 1981, Daman was presented the Boyce Sherrin Sportsmanship Award from the Cabarrus County Boys Club.

Benjamin started working for S&D Coffee in Concord after Johnson Motor Lines closed, and he eventually became the number-one coffee roaster. He retired from the company in 2006.

Daman continued his education in Cabarrus County schools and played basketball and football first at Concord Middle School and then football at Concord High. The rivalry between Concord High and A. L. Brown High in Kannapolis has gone on for many years. However, in 1986, Concord High won a football game against Kannapolis. The winning team was presented with a bell painted in the school's colors. Daman played center on the team and was delighted with the win to say the least.

During his junior year, his guidance counselor, Patricia Wood, asked him to apply for the Leadership Education and Development (LEAD) program for rising minority seniors hosted by colleges and universities across the country. Daman applied and was accepted, and the university he attended was UCLA. Expenses were paid for by the program. The students flew to their destinations on nonstop flights and were met by representatives of the program; they traveled the campuses together.

Before Daman graduated from Concord High in 1987, his counselor asked him to apply for the Bridge Program at the University of North Carolina at Chapel for six weeks of classes and to learn about college life; he had already been accepted at the university. The program helped incoming students to become acquainted with college life and classes. They received three hours credit as an elective, which became part of their academic records.

Daman graduated in 1991 from UNCC and then worked for Wachovia Bank for two years until he decided to find a job in Atlanta; he went to work there for CNN, which had entities other than news and sports. There were small companies at CNN that needed personnel to manage finances and answer calls requesting TV satellites.

In 1996, Daman decided he was ready to pursue an MBA. He was accepted at Duke University in Durham, North Carolina, and graduated in 1998.

═══ CHAPTER 15 ═══

Turning Points in an Integrated Society

As the 1970s began, more African American students received scholarships—academic and athletic—to attend predominately white colleges and universities. The faculties at those institutions were more integrated as well, and they were asked to become a part of mentoring groups to help minority student adjust to their new environments.

There was and still is even now a gap between the two races for scores that are represented as percentages. However, we knew then as well as now that black students are outnumbered by whites making the percentages for blacks lower. As of the latter part of the twentieth century and now the twenty-first century, there is a three-way comparison between whites, blacks, and Latinos. The test results now show both ethnic groups still have lower scores. However, there are and have always been a small majority of students who tend to resist working up to their academic potential for a plethora of reasons.

We did not have as much resistance during the 1970s, 1980s, and 1990s to educational achievement as we do today. Students with learning disabilities became more prevalent, and their needs had to be met. Special education classes were established after teachers became certified. Many students dropped out of school because they did not want their friends to know they would be in special ed classes. By the same token, students who were identified as gifted and talented were not always accepted by average students.

The main reason one-story schools have been built in the last thirty years was to accommodate students with physical disabilities; school systems did not want to pay for elevators and have to maintain them. However, new schools built in this century are multistoried, and elevators are included. Some school systems have designated schools as elementary, intermediate, middle, and high school. This requires more buses and longer school days. Students have to get to their bus stops earlier in the morning, and they get home later in the day because of the distances they must travel.

During the 1970s, black people became more open about how they viewed themselves, and they displayed their self-confidence openly. We began to take more pride in being black and accepted the heritage that went with it. The song "I'm Black and I'm Proud" written and recorded by the late James Brown helped us feel even better about ourselves as African Americans including those in low- to median-income levels. Students who were graduating from colleges and universities had better opportunities for employment. African American employment increased, and many black people became principals, lawyers, judges, doctors, firefighters, police officers, detectives, professional athletes, and entered many other professions they had been denied during segregation. Families were determined to present themselves as responsible citizens who were not interested in revenge but in proving their self-worth and willingness to work for the respect of whites.

At the university level, institutions were required to assemble a more diverse student population by establishing goals and timetables for the full utilization of educational opportunities for minorities and women by way of directives from the Department of Health, Education, and Welfare.

Prior to the fall of 1972, universities had not made racial or ethnic integration a top priority in awarding admission. Since there were so few racial and ethnic minority students who received PhDs, faculty jobs were hardly affected by these changes though an increasing numbers of women were receiving PhDs.

With the secretary of labor's revised order Number 4, universities were required to perform more-diligent searches to find equally qualified minority and women PhDs. Employers were obligated to follow Affirmative Action Title VII, which prohibited discrimination in hiring when a company or business employed fifteen or more workers. The Equal Employment Opportunity Office received and investigated complaints filed by those who had been discriminated against in hiring.

Alex Haley worked for many years researching the history of the Africans who were brought to this county and enslaved. His book *Roots* was published in 1974, and a made-for-TV movie was based on it. We as a people began vigorous research of the heritage that had been taken from slaves and other ancestors. The African names of slaves were taken from them and they were given the names of plantation owners.

Their African names probably could not be pronounced by whites during those years, but Africans did not have names such as Smith, Blake, Grant, Williams, Alexander, Haley, or Coleman.

After reading *Roots* and watching the movie, African Americans developed a stronger sense of self-pride. We also began searching for more books to become more familiar with our ancestors and their customs. This also led to the discovery of the African celebration of Kwanzaa, which begins on December 26 each year.

Other ways African Americans began to embrace their heritage included women wearing their hair naturally rather than pressing it with a hot iron and curling it. Men wore Afros. Many blacks began wearing dashikis in recognition of their heritage.

In 1972, Concord experienced civil unrest when the white proprietor of a convenience store and Laundromat on Polk Avenue and a black male got involved in an altercation. The black male was shot by the white male; he was wounded but did not die. When neighbors heard about the incident, rioting began. The proprietor had to leave the area for safety reasons without his car, which was set afire. His store and Laundromat were looted and burned. Then rental houses owned by the manager of the local Belk Department Store were set afire. However, those who were setting those houses on fire did not want homes owned by black people to burn, so they used water hoses to keep them wet. Other white-owned stores in the neighborhood were also burned. Once the community became settled again, we continued moving forward, taking advantage of better opportunities in employment and education.

However, another incident of civil unrest occurred in

Concord one night in July 1993. A group of young black adults stopped at the Waffle House Restaurant on Highway 29 North. A disturbance started for some reason among the group that prompted the manager to call the Concord Police Department for officers to disperse the crowd.

Two white officers were trying to arrest a black male, Angelo Robinson. He was pepper-sprayed, subdued, and placed in a patrol car. He was transported to the police station and was having trouble breathing before he was taken to jail. When the officers reached the Cabarrus County Jail, he was not responding. He was pronounced dead at Cabarrus Memorial Hospital (now Northeast Medical Center).

As the result of both tragic incidents, two human relations commissions were established. The one created after the 1972 disturbance had closed several years prior to the 1993 tragedy. In June 1992, a group of men began discussing underlying concerns about the racial health of Cabarrus County. Alderman Robert Lee Mathis helped found the Cabarrus County Human Relations Committee under the auspices of the Concord-Cabarrus Chamber of Commerce. Thomas Ramseur, the president and CEO of the chamber, played a significant role along with thirty or more others. During the second meeting of the group, Mathis said the men realized they had committed the cardinal sin of not involving women. "So we brought some ladies in, and they offered stability and common sense," Mathis said.

I was the first female he asked to attend a meeting to see whether I would be interested. When I went to the next meeting, we discussed the matter and decided we needed a human relations committee, and I was elected its chair.

Dr. Joel O. Nwagbaraocha, president of Barber-Scotia

College, suggested that our meetings be held at the college. As word spread about the formation of committee, more people began attending the monthly meetings. Prior to the start of this committee, there had been two murders, and a group had decided to form a committee called the Logan Community Association to help alleviate rumors; the human relations committee welcomed input from them as well. Others were a cross section of businesspeople, ministers, and interested citizens, black and white, who were concerned about the lack of communication between races.

One of the first things we did was to look at our own racial perceptions. Members of the committee openly discussed cultural differences and our experiences with racism. There were heated discussions at times, but we learned from one another and became comfortable working together. Committee members participated in diversity workshops. The committee sponsored two open-dialogue programs in the early part of 1993, and they went over very well with those in attendance. We had a panel of people with diverse backgrounds—black and white, younger and older—who spoke about their experiences with racism.

Our committee sponsored a bus tour through minority-populated areas so people could see the housing conditions and the need for help to make changes. The riot that ensued after the death of Angelo Darcel Robinson, who died in police custody, gave the human relations committee a sense of urgency. During the state of emergency, a rumor-control hotline was set up at the chamber of commerce with the permission of Thomas Ramseur, CEO. Television stations covering the unrest announced the existence of the hotline to help dispel rumors of more trouble in the neighborhood.

We were in constant contact with the police to find out what was going.

Robert Cansler, the chief of police then, was very much on board with the human relations committee and its importance to Concord and Cabarrus County from the beginning. Most people believed that had it not been for our efforts to control rumors, there would have been more problems.

North Carolina has a human relations commission. William Oxendine, a representative from North Carolina's Human Resources Commission, assisted us during the months of tension. Our committee was nominated for and received the David Coltrane Award given to volunteer committees.

In 1994, members of the human relations committee considered establishing a commission as a part of the city and county or as a nonprofit organization. That occurred, but the commission lasted for only about two years. Concord has not had any other incidents of civil disruption since 1993.

While serving as chairman of the community relations committee, I was asked to become involved in other organizations and boards. The first was the Juvenile Criminal Justice Committee for Cabarrus County. It oversaw funding for social service organizations to help juveniles stay out of trouble and in school.

I also served on the board of directors of the Concord/ Cabarrus Chamber of Commerce from 1995 to 1997 before it merged with the Kannapolis Chamber of Commerce. In 1996, I was appointed to serve on the Concord Planning and Zoning Commission, and I served two terms there. I learned how local governments work, and I found it very interesting.

In 2003, Wayne Troutman of Troutman Enterprises submitted my name to the Office of the Governor of North

Carolina for the North Carolina Marriage and Family Therapy Licensure Board. I was appointed by Governor Michael K. Easley and served two terms. In 2015, I became a member of the Cabarrus County Planning and Zoning Commission. I was asked to serve on the Cabarrus Family Medicine Board of Directors in 2004. The board was preparing to apply for federal funding to help people find affordable health care.

ABOUT THE AUTHOR

I want people to know that though there are differences between black and white people, they are far outweighed by the likenesses. Africans and their African American descendants are the only people who were originally brought to this country against their will. Consequently  they have been and to a certain extent are still denied complete civil rights. All other people who make up the melting pot of America migrated here for freedom that was not as they desired in Europe and other countries. Africans were forced to leave their country and the freedom they enjoyed for imprisonment in a country that valued only their labor.

Black Americans bleed the same blood types as whites, cry the same kind of tears when sad or hurt, have the same needs for food, shelter, currency and education. Most importantly we have the same capacity to think, learn, love and pray as our white counterparts. The color of our skin sets us apart from other races or nationalities of people, and for that we do not apologize.